Cowboy Slang

for Modern Day Use

Ricky Adams

Cowboy Slang
for Modern Day Use
Ricky Adams

Published by Cowpoke Press
TikTok @cowboysalng

ISBN: 9798869347527
Printed in the United States of America
1st Edition

Saddle up, partner, and learn some cowboy slang. Were you aware that cowboys in the 1800s had a distinct slang all their own? Most of these words have vanished from the English language. It's about time we start including these back into our everyday conversations. Whether you aim to amaze your friends, family, and colleagues, or channel the essence of a character from your cherished cowboy-themed video game, or simply desire to inject some style into your everyday discussions, developing fluency in cowboy slang will elevate your authenticity and reveal your inner cowboy.

Ace-High

-High regard-

"I was ace-high at my last job, but this new corporate waste land has drained me of all my professional accolades."

Adam's Ale

-Water-

"Man, that CrossFit workout kicked my butt! I had to drink so much Adam's ale to get through it, and I'm still thirsty"

"Did you see Larry´s last email, boy was he Airin´ the lungs. He better hope HR doesn´t see that."

Acknowledge the Corn

-To Confess-

"Come on man, it's time to acknowledge the corn. I know you used my skateboard. It was brand new and now the decks all scratched up!"

Apple-pie Order

-In top shape-

"Did you finish your book report?"

"Sure did! Finished it last night it's all in apple-pie order, and I'm fin to get a B to B+ for sure."

Bag of Nails

-Full of confusion-

"What your saying is a bag of nails! Of course you can't put diesel into an unleaded car..."

Ballyhoo

-Exaggeration-

"Helena really gave us the ballyhoo about how hard it was to fix that copier machine. I don't even want to use it anymore."

Bangtail

-A wild horse-

"I miss my old 2 door, stick shift, 1995 hooptie. It was a piece, but man, it was a total bangtail when you got it out on the open road."

Barkin´ at a Knot

-Doing something impossible-

˝Lumbergh asked me to finish the quarterly financial report before lunch but that´s barkin´ at a knot…there´s no way I´ll finish it in time.˝

Bee in Your Bonnet

-An idea-

"Seems like you have yourself a bee in your bonnet? I sure hope so because I have no idea how to fix this. "

Beef Tea

-Puddles that cows have been in-

"I can tell you didn't clean the shower. Look! It looks like there's beef tea all over the floor. Get back in here and clean it up!"

Boodle

-A crowd-

"Lets steer clear of that beach, there's a boodle of tourists there."

Bronc Buster

-Cowboy who could tame a wild horse-

"Why don't you have the new guy train with Jim. He seems a little wild, and Jim is a certified Bronc Buster. That guy will be your standard mindless corporate droid by the end of the week."

Buckaroo

-A cowboy-

"That classy buckaroo at table 3 tipped me fifty bucks!!"

Buffaloed

-Confused-

"Mrs Robbins really buffaloed me in class today with all that quantum physics mumbo-jumbo."

Corral Dust
-Tall tales-

"I can't listen to anymore of that corral dust, and I frankly don't care anymore about the Bigfoot hunt."

Cowpoke

-Lower ranking cowboy-

"Woah, slow down there cowpoke. The crosswalk clearly has 3 seconds left on it."

Doughgods

-Biscuits-

"Oh boy, I went to that Doughgods spot on 23rd Ave. It was so good, and the gravy was top notch!"

Dyed In The Wool

-Ingrained-

"I've played this gosh darn video game so much that the map of the land is dyed in the wool of my mind."

Eatin Irons

-Silverware-

"Excuse me, but can I bother you good sir for some eatin irons?"

Fine as
Cream Gravy

-Very good-

"Wow you look beautiful! That dress is as fine as cream gravy!"

Get a Wiggle On

-To hurry up-

"Get a wiggle on Karen! There's no one in line for the coaster with the 5 loops in it. I want to go on that one first!"

Hair Case
-Hat-

"Why do you always wear that hair case?
Honestly Karen, your hair cut isn't that...bad."

Hangfire

-To delay-

"Hangfire on getting that taxi, I just ordered more wings! "

Hit the Hay

-To go to bed-

"We've been driving literally all day. I'm beat, it's really time to hit the hay."

Lally-cooler

-A person who is successful-

"Did you hear about Georgie, he's a big internet lally-cooler now. He had some dance video go viral."

Music Root

-Sweet potato-

"I got wedge music root fries with my burger. They were totally delicious. I highly suggest them."

Namby-pamby
-Weak-

"Would you like room for cream and sugar?"

"No thank you. I prefer my coffee black. None of that namby-pamby sugary coffee."

Necessary
-Bathroom-

"Well I fell for the cheesy hot dogs at the gas station once again, and Dude, I will need to use your necessary immediately."

Nothing to Nobody

-Nobody's business-

"What I got for my bonus this year is nothing to nobody!"

Of the First Water

-First class-

"This album is of the first water. There is no way he'll ever be able to top this."

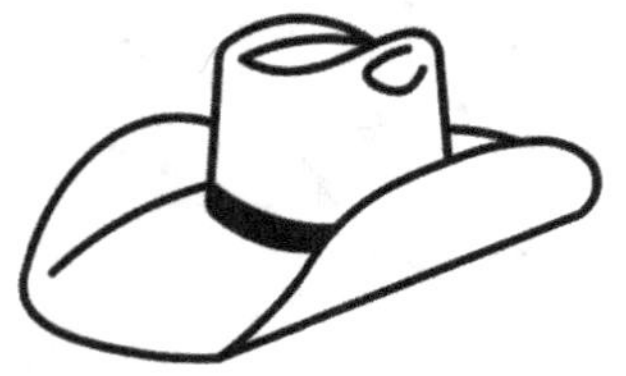

Old Rats

-One of the boys-

"Oh man, give Tommy a break. He's old rats. We used to hang back in the day."

One-horse

-Small-

"Nah don't go to that waterpark, its a one-horse waterpark. They only have like one decent slide, and it's always closed."

Outhouse

-Outside bathroom-

"I'm personally used to an outhouse, but this indoor toilet room is cool too I guess."

Overland Trout

-Bacon-

"Mmm Mmm I love the smell of the overland trout sizzling when I walk into Mama's kitchen."

Persnickity

-Picky-

"No, sorry we don't have mustard. My brother is very persnickity about the types of condiments we keep in the fridge."

Piddle

-Waste of time-

"I piddled around on the internet all day trying to figure out how to jailbreak my phone, and now my phone doesn't work at all…so you'll have to DM me because I'm not getting texts."

Pop Your Corn

-Speak your mind-

"Well now, we all want to hear what you have to say. Go on, pop your corn!"

Poppet

-Term of endearment-

"Aw poppet you had a hard day. Sit down and relax, I'll take care of dinner."

Post the Pony

-Pay up-

"Listen, I won this round of Bones. It's time to post the pony Buster!"

Pray Tell

-Tell me-

"What did corporate say about extending our PTO? Come on now, pray tell."

Rootin'-Tootin'

-Loudly exciting-

"Karaoke with the homies last night sure was a rootin-tootin' good time!"

Sand

-Toughness-

"That UFC fighter was pure sand. I can't believe the jabs he was taking in that last fight."

See How The Cat Jumps

-Discovering a secret-

"You clearly ate the last donut, I see how the cat jumps. It's written all over your face."

Skedaddle

-Run away-

"I totally embarressed myself at that party last night. I had to skedaddle home early to save face."

Slower than molasses in January

-Very slow-

"Hey Boss, sorry I am late. Traffic was slower than molasses in January."

Wake Snakes

-Start a ruckus-

"Watch me Bro, I'm about to wake snakes at tonight's family game night. No way Grandma is wining again.

Wamble-Cropped

-Sick to the stomach-

"I'm straight up wamble-cropped. I now know why those cheesy hotdogs were on sale for a buck. Terrible purchase!"